I CAN READ ABOUT

GOOD MANNERS

Written by Erica Frost

Illustrated by William Krasnoborski

Troll Associates

It is easy to have good manners. You don't have to read a lot of books or go to special schools.

If you are not sure how to behave, just ask yourself this question: *Am I being thoughtful of others?*

If the answer is *no*, try to act some other way.

But if the answer is *yes*, it is a sure sign that your manners are good.

Now let's pretend . . .

Suppose you just sat
down for breakfast.
A clean napkin is
folded at your place.
What do you do?

1. Put the napkin on your head
because you are always
chilly in the morning.

2. Tie the napkin over your nose, like a bandit, and have a shoot-out with your sister. (That way, you can start off the morning with a bang.)

3. Unfold your napkin halfway and put it in your lap.

You are about to eat
a piece of bread.
You want the butter
but it is on the other
side of the table.
What do you do?

1. Teach your dog to fetch.
Then say:

2. Tilt the table,

so the butter will slide over by itself.

3. Ask the person nearest to it
   to please pass the butter.

You are eating spaghetti in a restaurant. You are trying very hard to be neat, but the spaghetti keeps slipping off your fork.

What do you do?

1. Pick up the plate and *zloop up* the spaghetti. Try not to be noisy.

2. Lift it, very carefully,
   piece by piece, with
   your hands.

3. Twirl it around your fork, a
   little at a time, using your
   spoon to help.

You are at a
birthday party.
Someone offers you
a piece of cake.
What do you do?

1. Take two pieces because it is your
   best friend's party.

2. Take the biggest
   piece on the plate.

3. Take whichever piece is closest to you.

You have been invited to supper at your grandmother's house. She comes in, carrying a big bowl of mashed turnips. You hate turnips!

What do you do?

1. Put on your hat and coat and go home!

2. Grab your throat
   and look as if
   you are going
   to be sick.

3. Smile a wicked smile,
   and say:

4. Ask for just a little bit and try a tiny taste.
   Or say, "No thank you,"
   if you have an understanding grandma.

1. Jump up and down and shout.

You are in school.
Your teacher has just
asked a question
and you know
the answer.
What do you do?

2. Stand on your desk and call out
   the answer in a loud, deep voice.

3. Raise your hand and
   wait for your teacher
   to call on you.

1. Run through the halls and shout *hello* to everyone you see.

HELLO!

Your teacher has sent you on an errand to the principal's office. It is the first day of spring and you are in a wonderful mood. What do you do?

3. Walk cheerfully but quietly through the halls and return to your classroom as soon as you can.

2. Dance through the halls and shout *hello* only to the people you know.

The lunch bell just rang but your teacher is still talking. What do you do?

1. Run out the door yelling, "I'm free. I'm free."

2. Ask your friend if he wants
   to trade half a pickle
   for an oatmeal cookie.

3. Sit quietly in your seat until your teacher dismisses you.

You are playing in the schoolyard
with your friend. Both of you
find a ring with a pretty diamond
in it.
What do you do?

1. You keep it because
   you lost your own
   ring last week.

2. Your friend keeps
   it because she
   loves diamonds.

3. You *both* sell it, and divide the money.

4. Give it to a teacher or take it to the lost and found.

School is over and
you just got home.
What do you do?

1. Throw your coat and books on the
floor and yell, "I'm hungry."

2. Toss your coat and books
   to your mother
   and yell,

I'M HUNGRY!

3. Say hello to whoever is at home.

Put your coat and books away.

Then, (you guessed it) say . . . . . .

Your new friend is visiting for the first time. She does
not know anyone in your family.
What do you do?

1. Take her right
   to your room,
   and tell your
   brother to
   keep out
   if he knows
   what's good
   for him.

2. Introduce her by saying:

You are being introduced to someone for the first time.
What do you say?

1.

2.

3. SAY, "HELLO, HOW ARE YOU?"

The telephone rings
and you answer it.
What do you say?

1. BARNEY'S BAKERY, WHICH CRUMB DO YOU WANT TO SPEAK TO?

You have been invited to spend
a weekend at your friend's house.
You want to be a good guest.

What do you do?

1. Tell the family what games you want
   to play, what foods you want to eat,
   and what time you think they should
   all go to bed.

2. Explore the house
room by room.
Open every drawer
and door,

especially the one to
the refrigerator.

3. Try to enjoy what the family has planned for you.

And remember to say *"Please"* and *"Thank You."*
Being thoughtful is what good manners is all about.

There will be other times
when you will have to decide
how to behave.

But, if you stop

and ask yourself, "Am I being thoughtful of others?"—

—you will always know how to act.

And, what's more, you will always be welcome—
anytime, anyplace.